THE LAND OF JUDEA, JUST OUTSIDE JERUSALEM, ON THE ROAD TO BETHLE
BECAUSE OF A CENSUS ORDERED BY ROMAN OFFICIALS, PEOPLE ALL OVER JUDEA MUST RETURN TO THEIR ANCESTRAL HOMES.
AMONG THOSE MANY TRAVELERS ARE MARY AND HER HUSBAND JOSEPH.

THEIR DESTINATION IS BETHLEHEM, EIGHTY MILES TO HE SOUTH OF THEIR HOME IN NAZARETH.
MARY, LET'S STOP. JUST FOR A MOMENT.
I'M FINE, JOSEPH.
WE WANT TO MAKE GOOD TIME.

NORMALLY, THE JOURNEY WOULD TAKE JUST FOUR OR FIVE DAYS, BUT MARY IS EXPECTING A CHILD.
BETHLEHEM ISN'T GOING ANYWHERE. IT'LL STILL BE THERE WHEN WE ARRIVE.
YES, AND ALL THESE PEOPLE WILL ALSO BE THERE WHEN WE ARRIVE!

DON'T WORRY. I HAVE RELATIVES THERE.
WE'LL STAY IN AN INN UNTIL WE CAN TRACK THEM DOWN. EVERYTHING WILL BE FINE.

AS SHE HAS DONE MANY TIMES OVER THE LAST FEW MONTHS, MARY FINDS HERSELF REFLECTING ON WHAT HAS BROUGHT HER TO THIS MOMENT.
I KNOW, JOSEPH. I KNOW.

LUKE 2:1-4

AS A YOUNG WOMAN IN THE SMALL VILLAGE OF NAZARETH, SHE EXPECTED AN UNEVENTFUL AND TRADITIONAL LIFE.
SHE AND HER HUSBAND JOSEPH WERE BETROTHED, MEANING THEY HAD BEEN BOUND TOGETHER IN THE MARRIAGE CONTRACT.
BUT THEY STILL LIVED APART FROM EACH OTHER, WITH THEIR OWN FAMILIES.

FOLLOWING TRADITION, THEY BOTH WAITED FOR THE NIGHT THAT JOSEPH'S FATHER WOULD SEND HIM TO GET MARY.
THEN THERE WOULD BE A SECOND, EVEN BIGGER CEREMONY.
AND JOSEPH WOULD TAKE MARY HOME WITH HIM TO BE HIS BRIDE.

MARY! I SAW JOSEPH WORKING ON YOUR NEW HOME YESTERDAY!
YOUR PARENTS WERE WISE TO MARRY YOU TO A CARPENTER!
HE'S A GOOD MAN!
THAT HE IS!

THEIR LIFE TOGETHER WOULD BEGIN.
MARY KNEW THAT JOSEPH, A HARD WORKER AND GODLY MAN, WOULD MAKE FOR A WONDERFUL HUSBAND AND FATHER.

THEY PLANNED TO LIVE IN THE HOUSE JOSEPH BUILT NEAR HIS FAMILY'S NAZARETH HOME, FILL IT WITH CHILDREN, AND GROW OLD TOGETHER.
BUT THOSE WERE THE PLANS OF A YOUNG MAN AND WOMAN, AND THOSE PLANS WERE ABOUT TO CHANGE DRAMATICALLY.

GREETINGS, MARY . . .

LUKE 1:26-28

WHAT... WHAT DO YOU WANT...
YOU HAVE NOTHING TO FEAR, MARY!
INDEED, YOU HAVE FOUND FAVOR WITH GOD!
YOU WILL SOON BECOME PREGNANT AND GIVE BIRTH TO A SON.
AND YOU WILL GIVE HIM THE NAME JESUS.

LUKE 1:28-31

ME?
YES.
YOU.

HE WILL BE CALLED SON OF THE MOST HIGH!
THE LORD GOD WILL GIVE HIM THE THRONE OF KING DAVID, FROM WHOM YOU ARE DESCENDED, AND HE WILL REIGN OVER THE HOUSE OF JACOB FOREVER!
BUT...

LUKE 1:32-37

MARY'S LIFE WAS NOT THE ONLY LIFE TO BE DISRUPTED BY THE ANGEL'S NEWS.
JOSEPH! I NEED TO SPEAK TO YOU!
MARY!
LOOK! I'VE FIGURED OUT WHERE WE WILL BUILD ON WHEN WE HAVE CHILDREN!
AND I NEED TO KNOW WHERE YOU WANTED THE FIRE PIT!

WHAT'S WRONG, MARY?
DON'T WORRY, I'LL HAVE THIS PLACE PRE-PARED IN TIME FOR OUR MARRIAGE CEREMONY!
JOSEPH, I'M NOT WORRIED ABOUT THAT... I HAVE SOMETHING IMPORTANT TO TELL YOU.

AND SO, JOSEPH LISTENED AS SHE OLD HIM EVERYTHING.
...AND I CARRY THE BABY NOW, JOSEPH.

YOU EXPECT ME TO BELIEVE THIS?

I HAVE SPENT SO MUCH TIME AND STRENGTH BUILDING THIS HOUSE FOR YOU AND FOR OUR CHILDREN...
GET OUT OF HERE, MARY.
PLEASE.

MATTHEW 1:18

SOON AFTERWARD, MARY WENT AWAY TO HER COUSIN ELIZABETH'S HOME IN JUDEA, A TOWN IN THE HILL COUNTRY OUTSIDE NAZARETH.
THANK YOU FOR WALKING WITH ME, ZACHARIAS.
IS ELIZABETH'S BABY... YOU'RE NOT GOING TO ANSWER ME, ARE YOU?

MARY! MY PRECIOUS LITTLE COUSIN!

HELLO, ELIZABETH.
ELIZABETH, IS SOMETHING WRONG WITH ZACHARIAS? HE DIDN'T SAY A WORD --
OOOH!
ELIZABETH! IS IT THE BABY?
YES! YES! BUT NOT LIKE YOU THINK!

AND ELIZABETH WAS FILLED WITH THE HOLY SPIRIT.
MARY, YOU ARE THE MOST BLESSED OF ALL WOMEN!
AND BLESSED IS THE CHILD IN YOUR WOMB!
BUT I, TOO, AM BLESSED! FOR I HAVE, STANDING IN MY OWN HOUSE, MY COUSIN, THE MOTHER OF MY LORD!

OH, ELIZABETH! HOW... HOW DID YOU KNOW?
MARY, AS SOON AS YOUR WORDS REACHED MY EARS, THE BABY IN MY OWN WOMB LEAPT FOR JOY!

WE HAVE MUCH TO TALK ABOUT...

LUKE 1:39-45

...SO I WAS VERY GLAD WHEN OU ASKED ME O COME HERE, ELIZABETH.
JOSEPH COULD HAVE DEMANDED THAT I BE STONED TO DEATH.
BUT HE THINKS A QUIET DIVORCE IS THE BEST WAY: HE'S NOT MARRYING AN ADULTERER, AND I CAN HAVE THE BABY AND LIVE WITH MY FAMILY.
HE IS A GOOD MAN, MARY. GIVE HIM TIME.

YOU ASKED IF ZACHARIAS WAS OKAY. DID YOU KNOW THAT HE, TOO, RECEIVED A VISIT FROM AN ANGEL?
ZACHARIAS AND I NEVER HAD CHILDREN, BUT NOT BECAUSE WE DIDN'T WANT THEM.
WE TRIED. WE PRAYED. WE GAVE UP.

"IT JUST WASN'T OUR LOT IN LIFE, WE DECIDED, TRUSTING GOD THAT THERE WAS A PURPOSE."
"BUT WHEN ZACHARIAS WAS IN JERUSALEM FOR HIS REGULAR DUTY AS A PRIEST, HE WAS SELECTED BY LOT TO GO INTO THE HOLY PLACE IN THE TEMPLE TO KEEP THE INCENSE BURNING."

"PRIESTS ENTER THE HOLY PLACE ALONE, BUT SUDDENLY MY ZACHARIAS FOUND HIM-SELF WITH A COMPANION!"
THERE IS NOTHING TO FEAR, ZACHARIAS.
YOUR PRAYERS HAVE BEEN ANSWERED. YOU AND YOUR WIFE ELIZABETH WILL SOON HAVE A SON.

YOU WILL GIVE HIM THE NAME JOHN AND HE WILL BRING JOY TO YOUR HOUSE.
MANY, MANY PEOPLE WILL REJOICE BECAUSE OF HIS BIRTH!

LUKE 1:5-14

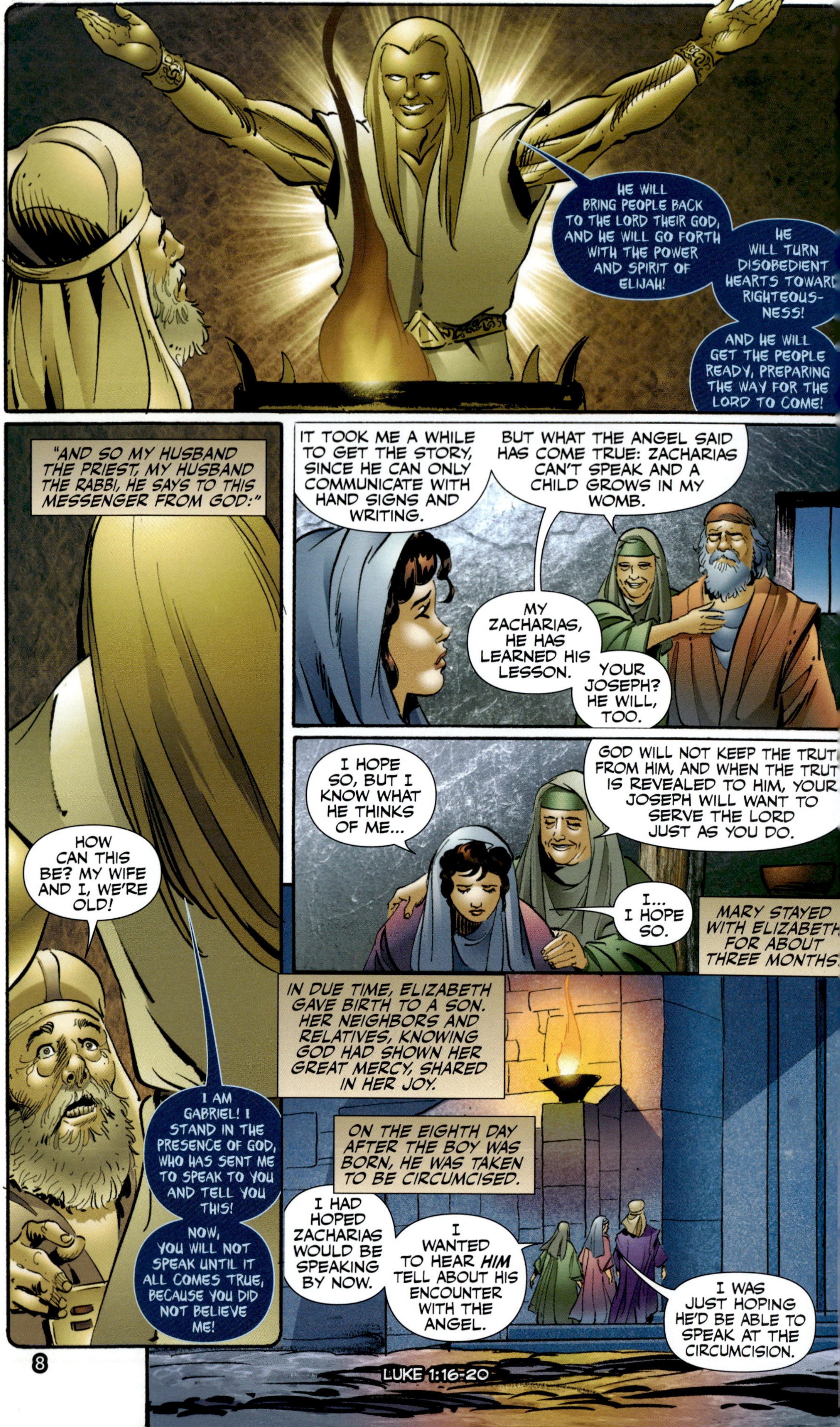

HE WILL BRING PEOPLE BACK TO THE LORD THEIR GOD, AND HE WILL GO FORTH WITH THE POWER AND SPIRIT OF ELIJAH!

HE WILL TURN DISOBEDIENT HEARTS TOWARD RIGHTEOUS-NESS!

AND HE WILL GET THE PEOPLE READY, PREPARING THE WAY FOR THE LORD TO COME!

"AND SO MY HUSBAND THE PRIEST, MY HUSBAND THE RABBI, HE SAYS TO THIS MESSENGER FROM GOD:"

HOW CAN THIS BE? MY WIFE AND I, WE'RE OLD!

I AM GABRIEL! I STAND IN THE PRESENCE OF GOD, WHO HAS SENT ME TO SPEAK TO YOU AND TELL YOU THIS!

NOW, YOU WILL NOT SPEAK UNTIL IT ALL COMES TRUE, BECAUSE YOU DID NOT BELIEVE ME!

IT TOOK ME A WHILE TO GET THE STORY, SINCE HE CAN ONLY COMMUNICATE WITH HAND SIGNS AND WRITING.

BUT WHAT THE ANGEL SAID HAS COME TRUE: ZACHARIAS CAN'T SPEAK AND A CHILD GROWS IN MY WOMB.

MY ZACHARIAS, HE HAS LEARNED HIS LESSON.

YOUR JOSEPH? HE WILL, TOO.

I HOPE SO, BUT I KNOW WHAT HE THINKS OF ME...

GOD WILL NOT KEEP THE TRUT FROM HIM, AND WHEN THE TRUT IS REVEALED TO HIM, YOUR JOSEPH WILL WANT TO SERVE THE LORD JUST AS YOU DO.

I... I HOPE SO.

MARY STAYED WITH ELIZABETH FOR ABOUT THREE MONTHS.

IN DUE TIME, ELIZABETH GAVE BIRTH TO A SON. HER NEIGHBORS AND RELATIVES, KNOWING GOD HAD SHOWN HER GREAT MERCY, SHARED IN HER JOY.

ON THE EIGHTH DAY AFTER THE BOY WAS BORN, HE WAS TAKEN TO BE CIRCUMCISED.

I HAD HOPED ZACHARIAS WOULD BE SPEAKING BY NOW.

I WANTED TO HEAR *HIM* TELL ABOUT HIS ENCOUNTER WITH THE ANGEL.

I WAS JUST HOPING HE'D BE ABLE TO SPEAK AT THE CIRCUMCISION.

LUKE 1:16-20

-- AND I PRESUME THE CHILD WILL BE NAMED ZACHARIAS, AFTER HIS FATHER.
NO!
JOHN! HIS NAME IS TO BE JOHN!

BUT THERE'S NO JOHN IN HIS FAMILY THAT I KNOW OF!
IS THERE A JOHN IN YOURS?
NO, BUT HE MUST BE NAMED JOHN!
SHOULDN'T YOU GIVE HIM A GOOD FAMILY NAME?

I DON'T THINK I KNOW ***ANYONE*** WITH THAT NAME!
ZACHARIAS, WHAT DO YOU THINK OF THIS?
SOMEONE PLEASE GET ZACHARIAS A WRITING TABLET!

HIS NAME IS JOHN.

VERY WELL, THEN, JOHN IT IS!
AH! PRAISE THE LORD!!!

PRAISE THE LORD, FOR HE HAS REDEEMED HIS PEOPLE!
AND YOU, MY SON, WILL BE THE LORD'S PROPHET, PREPARING PEOPLE FOR THE LORD'S SALVATION AND FORGIVE-NESS!
AND EVERYONE IN THE AREA WAS FILLED WITH AWE AND TALKED ABOUT ALL THAT HAD HAPPENED WITH ZACHARIAS AND ELIZABETH.

LUKE 1:59-64

MATTHEW 1:19-20

MATTHEW 1:20-25

AFTER MARY CAME HOME FROM HE
COUSIN'S HOUSE, AND AFTER JOSE
COMPLETED THE WORK ON THEIR HOM
THE HOUR ARRIVED WHEN JOSEPH'
FATHER SENT HIM TO GET HIS BRIDE

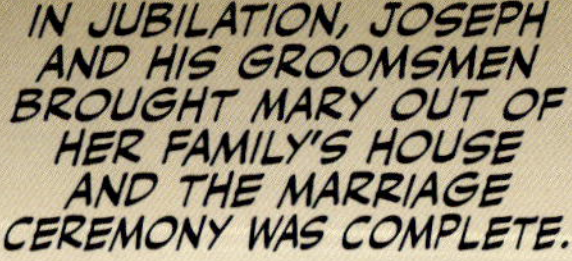

BUT JOSEPH HAD NO UNION WITH HER. HE WOULD WAIT UNTIL AFTER HER PROMISED SON WAS BORN.

LUKE 1:57-58; MATTHEW 1:24-25

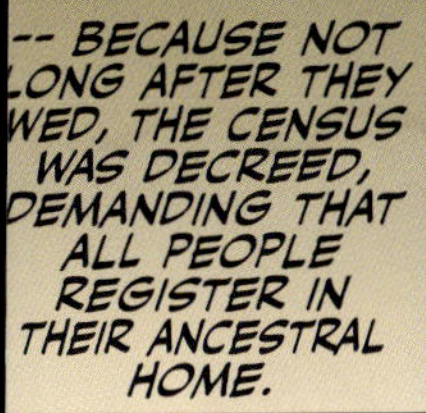

AND THE BIRTHPLACE OF THIS CHILD AS WELL. WE NEED TO GET A PLACE TO STAY, JOSEPH.

AND SOON.

WE'LL HAVE A WARM BED TONIGHT AND CONNECT WITH MY FAMILY TOMORROW.

AND THEY WERE HAPPY TO FOLLOW THE PATH TOGETHER.

LUKE 2:1-5

JERUSALEM.
KING HEROD!

YOU ARE GENERAL QUIRINIUS' ENVOY, YES?
WELCOME! HOW MAY I SERVE YOU?
GOVERNOR QUIRINIUS WANTS TO KNOW HOW THE CENSUS FARES, KING HEROD.

GENERAL QUIRINIUS IS GOVERNOR OF SYRIA, BUT --
MAKE NO MISTAKE, KING HEROD, GENERAL QUIRINIUS MAY NOT BE GOVERNOR OF JUDEA --
-- BUT HE DOES GOVERN OVER YOU.
REPORT TO GENERAL QUIRINIUS THAT NAUGHT HAS CHANGED SINCE LAST HE SENT AN ENVOY TO CHECK IN ON ME.

PEOPLE ARE GOING TO THEIR HOMETOWNS AS ROME HAS REQUIRED, BUT THERE ARE SMALL REBELLIONS AND UPRISINGS HERE AND THERE.
HIS ORDER HAS USED UP MUCH OF THE GOOD-WILL I HAVE WITH THESE PEOPLE.

HMMMM...
THE CENSUS SERVES A PURPOSE.
IT SHOWS WHO IS AND WHO IS NOT LOYAL TO ROME AND, I GUESS, TO YOU AS WELL.

THE UPRISINGS YOU REFER TO GIVE US OPPORTUNITY TO MEASURE WHAT REBELLIONS AGAINST ROME FROM YOUR REGION MIGHT LOOK LIKE.
YOU NEGLECTED TO REPORT THAT IT IS LOOKING LIKE THE PHARISEES IN YOUR REGION HAVE NO PLANS TO TAKE PART IN THE CENSUS.

LUKE 2:1-2

THE CENSUS IS NOT OVER.
YOU CAN TELL GENERAL QUIRINIUS THAT ALL GOES WELL.
AND YOU CAN TELL HIM THAT HE NEED NOT SEND HIS LAPDOGS TO CHECK ON ME.
COME.
HAVE YOU HEARD THE JOKE CAESAR TELLS ABOUT THIS KING HEROD?
SIR?
"I'D RATHER BE A PIG IN HEROD'S HOUSE THAN ONE OF HIS SONS," CAESAR SAYS.
HEROD PRETENDS TO BE JEWISH BY NOT EATING PORK, HOPING THE PEOPLE WILL EMBRACE HIM.
BUT HE'S FED HIS OWN FAMILY MEMBERS TO HIS CROCODILES BECAUSE HE FEARED THEY THREATENED HIS THRONE.
HE'D HAVE THROWN ME TO THE CROCODILES WERE I NOT AN OFFICIAL FROM ROME.
THAT IS A MAN WILLING TO DO ANYTHING TO KEEP HIS THRONE --
-- ANYTHING.

BETHLEHEM.
NIGHTFALL.
EVEN IF I KNEW WHERE TO LOOK FOR MY RELATIVES, I DOUBT I COULD FIND THEM ANYTIME SOON.
LET'S JUST FIND A PLACE TO STAY FOR THE NEXT FEW DAYS.
WE CAN FIND THEM LATER. I NEED -- AH! -- TO LIE DOWN.

THIS ISN'T WHAT I EXPECTED.
ARE YOU OKAY?
MY BACK IS JUST A LITTLE... UNCOMFORTABLE. LET'S FIND AN INN...

PLEASE SIR, DO YOU HAVE A ROOM FOR US?
DOES IT LOOK LIKE I HAVE A ROOM? I RENTED OUT BOTH OF THEM A WEEK AGO!

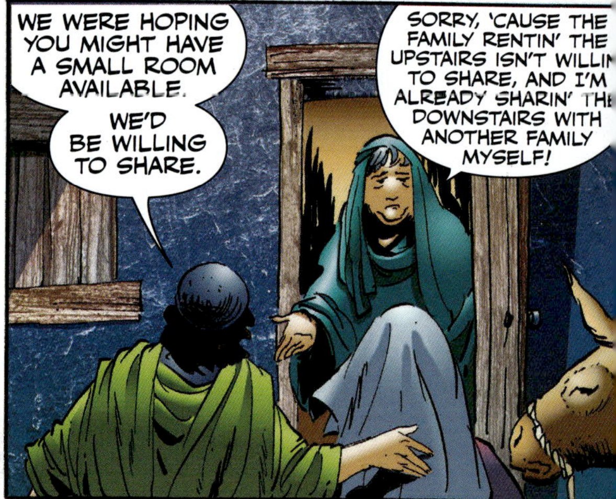
WE WERE HOPING YOU MIGHT HAVE A SMALL ROOM AVAILABLE.
WE'D BE WILLING TO SHARE.
SORRY, 'CAUSE THE FAMILY RENTIN' THE UPSTAIRS ISN'T WILLI TO SHARE, AND I'M ALREADY SHARIN' TH DOWNSTAIRS WITH ANOTHER FAMILY MYSELF!

HELLO! PLEASE COME!
LET'S GO, JOSEPH, THEY AREN'T GOING TO OPEN THE DOOR.
FROM THE SOUNDS IN THERE, THEY'VE GOT A FULL HOUSE.

PLEASE, SIR, NO ONE HAS ANY ROOM FOR US.
I'M SORRY!
WE JUST NEED A SHELTER. YOU SEE, MY WIFE --
YEAH! YOU BETTER FIND A PLACE SOON; SHE LOOKS READY TO BURST!

LUKE 2:6-7

IT'S NOT THE BEST ROOM IN BETHLEHEM.

BUT IT'LL KEEP YOU DRY AND IT'S CHEAP.

THANK YOU, SIR.

LUKE 2:6-7

OH!
BUT I SHOULDN'T LEAVE YOU ALONE!
THERE'S TIME, JOSEPH.
IT'S JUST STARTING, I THINK.
GO! BUT HURRY!

I'LL SEE IF THE INNKEEPER KNOWS OF ANYONE!
I'LL BE RIGHT BACK!

HEY!
MY WIFE!
WHAT'S GOING ON?

THE BABY IS COMING! WE NEED A MIDWIFE!
GET BACK IN THERE WITH YOUR WIFE!
I'LL FIND ONE!

THEY'LL BE HERE ANY MOMENT.
EVERY-THING WILL BE JUST FINE.
I KNOW.

LUKE 2:6

I FOUND SOME-ONE.
YOU'RE THE FATHER?
I'M HER HUSBAND.
YOU MEN SHOULDN'T BE IN HERE.

TAKE GOOD CARE OF THEM!
THAT'S A VERY SPECIAL CHILD!
YES, YES, WE KNOW.
YOU REALLY MUST GO NOW.
NOW, YOUNG LADY, TELL ME WHAT YOU'RE FEELING.

IT'S OKAY, YOU'RE DOING WELL.
IT'S TOO MUCH! I CAN'T!
HERE'S WHAT I WANT YOU TO DO NEXT TIME YOU FEEL PAIN COMING...

LUKE 2:7

SIR!
YOU HAVE A SON!

HE'S BEAUTIFUL.
YES. HE IS.

OUT IN THE NEARBY FIELDS, SHEPHERDS WATCHED THEIR FLOCK OF SHEEP.

GRAND-FATHER, DO WE REALLY ALL NEED TO BE OUT HERE?

IT'S COLD, AND I'M TIRED!

AH, TOBIN! HOW COULD YOU NOT LOVE BEING OUT HERE ON A NIGHT LIKE THIS!

WE SAFEGUARD THE MOST PRECIOUS OF CREATURES!

THESE SHEEP PROVIDE WOOL TO KEEP OUR PEOPLE WARM; MUTTON AND CHEESE TO KEEP OUR PEOPLE FED; MILK TO SALVE OUR PEOPLE'S THIRST!

KING DAVID HIMSELF WAS A SHEPHERD -- PERHAPS OUR FLOCK COULD BE TRACED BACK TO ONE OF HIS!

AND SOME OF THE LAMBS THESE EWES WILL GIVE BIRTH TO MAY EVEN BE USED AS A SACRIFICE FOR THE SINS OF --

WHAT'S GOING ON?

GRAND-FATHER, LOOK!

DO NOT BE AFRAID.

TODAY, IN THE TOWN OF BETHLEHEM, THE CITY OF DAVID, YOUR SAVIOR HAS BEEN BORN!

HE IS CHRIST THE LORD!

YOU WILL FIND HIM WRAPPED IN SWADDLING CLOTHS AND LYING IN A MANGER!

LUKE 2:13-14

GLORY TO GOD IN THE HIGHEST! ON EARTH, PEACE TO MEN ON WHOM HIS FAVOR RESTS!

EXCUSE ME...

WE WERE TOLD... THAT S, WE'VE BEEN INFORMED --
ANGELS TOLD US THAT THE BABY MESSIAH HAS BEEN BORN!

ANGELS?
ANGELS. SURPRISED?

THEY SAID THE BABY'D BE IN A MANGER, AND THIS IS THE ONLY MANGER WE'VE FOUND WITH A BABY!
WE'VE CHECKED THEM ALL!
IS THIS HIM?

YES.
WHAT'S HIS NAME?
JESUS.
IT MEANS...

LUKE 2:21

...THE LORD IS SALVATION.

THE MAGI'S STORY

"KINGMAKERS"

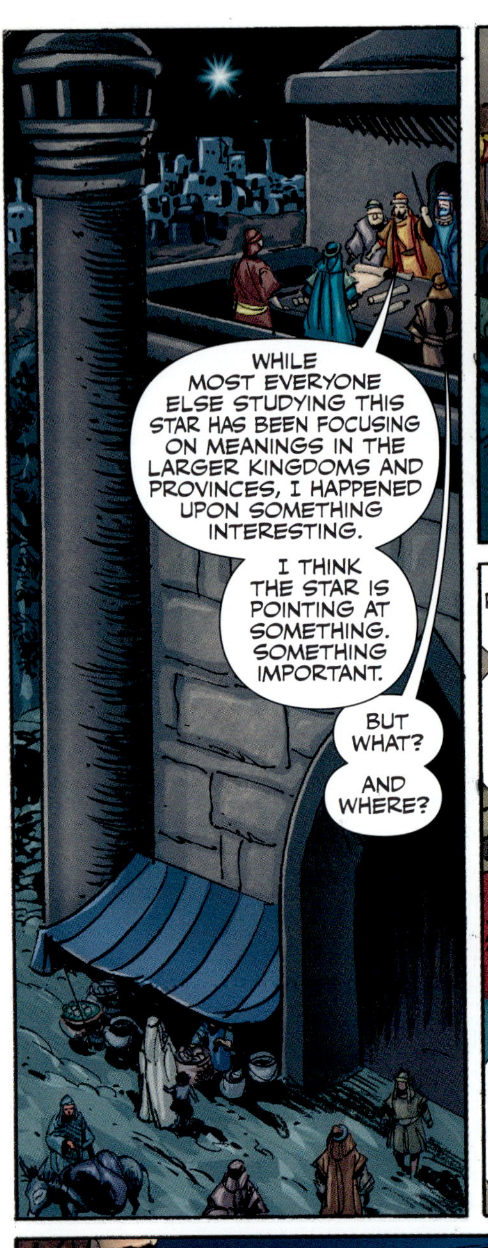
WHILE MOST EVERYONE ELSE STUDYING THIS STAR HAS BEEN FOCUSING ON MEANINGS IN THE LARGER KINGDOMS AND PROVINCES, I HAPPENED UPON SOMETHING INTERESTING.
I THINK THE STAR IS POINTING AT SOMETHING. SOMETHING IMPORTANT.
BUT WHAT?
AND WHERE?

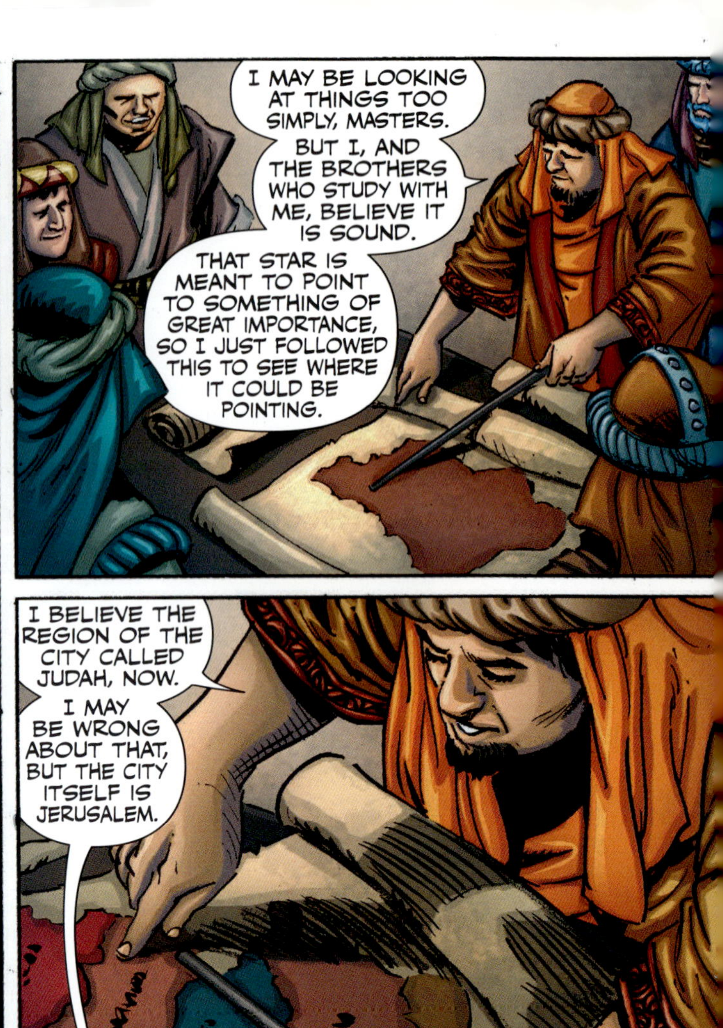
I MAY BE LOOKING AT THINGS TOO SIMPLY, MASTERS.
BUT I, AND THE BROTHERS WHO STUDY WITH ME, BELIEVE IT IS SOUND.
THAT STAR IS MEANT TO POINT TO SOMETHING OF GREAT IMPORTANCE, SO I JUST FOLLOWED THIS TO SEE WHERE IT COULD BE POINTING.
I BELIEVE THE REGION OF THE CITY CALLED JUDAH, NOW.
I MAY BE WRONG ABOUT THAT, BUT THE CITY ITSELF IS JERUSALEM.
IF WE WERE TO FOLLOW THIS STAR, FOLLOWING THIS LINE, IT WOULD TAKE US PAST A LARGE CITY IN THE SMALL NATION OF ISRAEL.

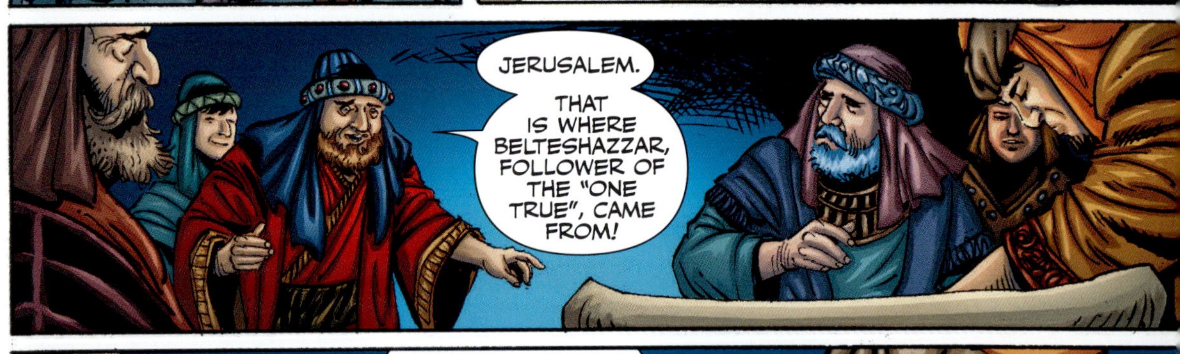
JERUSALEM.
THAT IS WHERE BELTESHAZZAR, FOLLOWER OF THE "ONE TRUE", CAME FROM!

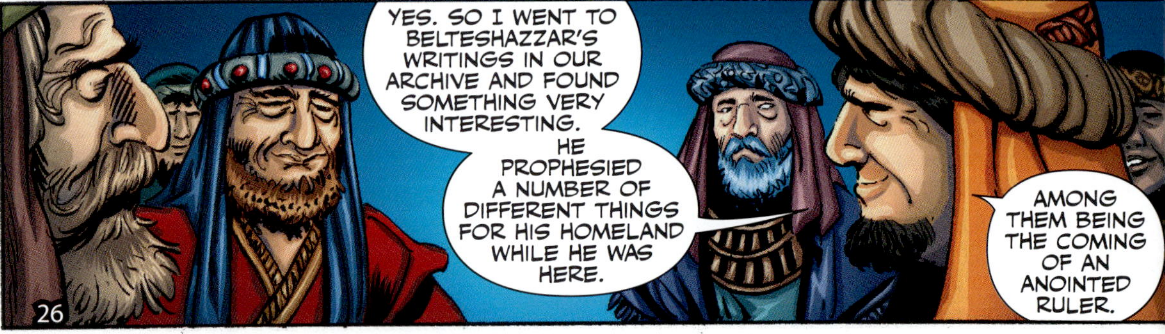
YES. SO I WENT TO BELTESHAZZAR'S WRITINGS IN OUR ARCHIVE AND FOUND SOMETHING VERY INTERESTING.
HE PROPHESIED A NUMBER OF DIFFERENT THINGS FOR HIS HOMELAND WHILE HE WAS HERE.
AMONG THEM BEING THE COMING OF AN ANOINTED RULER.

I CALCULATED WHAT I COULD
OM THE CALENDAR LTESHAZZAR USED, AND IT SEEMED REASONABLE TO SSUME THAT THIS STAR COULD BE RELATED TO THE COMING OF THAT "ANOINTED RULER".
ALL OF US HAVE WORKED RELESSLY TO CHECK ND DOUBLE CHECK HE POSSIBILITY THAT WE ARE CORRECT.
THE ANSWER TO THIS STAR WILL BE FOUND IN THE REGION AROUND JERUSALEM!

BALATHA, KURI, YOU AND YOUR BROTHERS HAVE PERFORMED ADMIRABLY.
YOU WILL NEED TO ACCUMULATE ALL THE WRITINGS OF BELTESHAZZAR AND ANY OTHER HEBREW WRITINGS WE MAY HAVE TO BRING WITH US SO WE MAY EXAMINE THEM IN TRANSIT.
"IN TRANSIT"? TO WHERE?
WE HAD ALREADY DETERMINED TO FOLLOW THIS STAR. YOU MAY HAVE DISCOVERED OUR DESTINATION!

AND SO WE SET OUT.

WE FOLLOWED THE STAR, BUT WE DID SO KNOWING WHAT OUR MOST LIKELY DESTINATION WOULD BE.

NIGHT AFTER NIGHT WE RODE ON.

UNTIL, ONE NIGHT...

JERUSALEM!

IT DID NOT TAKE LONG FOR MY MASTERS TO GAIN AUDIENCE WITH THE KING.

WE SEEK
HE NEWBORN
KING, KING
HEROD.
THE KING OF THE JEWS.
WE HAVE SEEN HIS STAR IN THE EAST.
AND WE COME TO WORSHIP HIM.
A NEWLY BORN KING? I WILL HAVE TO CONFER WITH MY SCHOLARS AND PRIESTS...
S WE WAITED I FELT OUBLY BAD FOR THE EOPLE OF THIS REGION.
TO HAVE EMPIRES RULE OVER THEM FOR SO LONG WAS BAD ENOUGH, BUT TO HAVE A KING LIKE THIS PLACED OVER THEM BY THOSE EMPIRES?
DON'T TELL ME WHAT YOU *DON'T* KNOW! TELL ME WHAT YOU *DO* KNOW!!!
TRAGIC.
FINALLY...
THE PROPHET MICAH HAS WRITTEN, "YOU, BETHLEHEM, IN JUDAH, ARE NOT LEAST AMONG THE RULERS OF JUDAH..."
"...FOR FROM YOU WILL COME A RULER WHO WILL BE THE SHEPHERD OF MY PEOPLE."
YOUR ANSWER, GOOD MAGI!
NOW, WHEN YOU DO FIND THIS CHILD, THIS KING, PLEASE, REPORT BACK TO ME SO I MIGHT ALSO GO TO HIM AND WORSHIP HIM.
ND SO, TO THE SMALL TOWN OF BETHLEHEM WE WENT, FOLLOWING THE STAR AS WE DID.
AS WE DREW CLOSER, QUESTIONS CLOUDED MY MIND.
AND WHEN WE ARRIVED, ONE QUESTION CAME TO THE FOREFRONT.
THIS WAS IT?

THIS WAS WHAT THE STAR HAD BEEN AN ORACLE TO?
A CHILD WHO LIVED IN SUCH A HUMBLE HOUSE... THE HOUSE OF A CARPENTER.
HE WOULD NOT SIT IN A THRONE, BUT RATHER IN A CHAIR HIS OWN FATHER WOULD BUILD!
BUT MY MASTERS KNEELED BEFORE THE CHILD AS IF HE WERE THE ROMAN EMPEROR HIMSELF!
AND EVEN AFTER SEEING THE CHILD AND THE CHILD'S LOW STATUS, THEY PRESENTED THE GIFTS THEY HAD BROUGHT:
GOLD, THE MOST PRECIOUS OF ALL METALS, USED TO CROWN KINGS IN PERSIA AND MANY OTHER NATIONS...
FRANKINCENSE, A PERFUME USED AS INCENSE IN MANY RELIGIOUS RITES...
AND MYRRH, A PERFUME USED IN THE EMBALMING OF THE DEAD OR EVEN AS AN OIL FOR ANOINTING...